OUR LIVING WORLD: EARTH'S BIOMES

Grasslands

Barbara A. Somervill

TRADITION BOOKS®, MAPLE PLAIN, MINNESOTA

A NEW TRADITION IN CHILDREN'S PUBLISHING™

Grasslands

volume 6

ABOUT THE AUTHOR

Barbara A. Somervill is the author

of many books for children. She loves

learning and sees every writing

project as a chance to learn new

information or gain a new under-

standing. Ms. Somervill grew up in

New York State, but has also lived in

Toronto, Canada; Canberra, Australia;

California; and South Carolina. She

currently lives with her husband in

Simpsonville, South Carolina.

CONTENT ADVISER

Susan Woodward, Professor of

Geography, Radford University,

Radford, Virginia

In gratitude to George R. Peterson Sr. for introducing me to the beauty of creation
—George R. Peterson Jr., Publisher, Tradition Books®

Published in the United States of America by Tradition Books® and distributed to the school
and library market by The Child's World®

[ACKNOWLEDGMENTS]
For Editorial Directions, Inc.: E. Russell Primm, Editorial Director; Dana Meachen Rau, Line
Editor; Katie Marsico, Associate Editor; Judi Shiffer, Associate Editor and Library Media
Specialist; Matthew Messbarger, Editorial Assistant; Susan Hindman, Copy Editor; Lucia
Raatma, Proofreaders; Ann Grau Duvall, Peter Garnham, Deborah Grahame, Katie
Marsico, Elizabeth K. Martin, and Kathy Stevenson, Fact Checkers; Tim Griffin/IndexServ,
Indexer; Cian Loughlin O'Day, Photo Researcher; Linda S. Koutris, Photo Selector

For The Design Lab: Kathleen Petelinsek, design, art direction, and cartography;
Kari Thornborough, page production

[PHOTOS]
Cover/frontispiece: Layne Kennedy/Corbis.
Interior: ABPL/Animals Animals/Earth Scenes: 81 (Richard Du Toit), 82 (Keith Begg);
Animals Animals/Earth Scenes: 11 (Dominique Braud), 26 (Erwin & Peggy Bauer), 34
(McDonald Wildlife Photography), 41 (Bruce Davidson), 42 (Mike Holmes), 43 (Michael
Gadomski), 47 (D. Allen Photography), 49 (Bertram G. Murray), 52 (C. C. Lockwood), 58
(Richard Shiell), 59 (Mago World Image), 63 (J. & B. Photographers), 68 (Mark Chappell),
74 (Norbert Rosing), 86 (Lynn Stone), 89 (Azure Computer & Photo Services); Fred
Atwood: 17, 54; Brand X Pictures/Punchstock: 4; Corbis: 6 (Tim Wright), 12 (Hubert
Stadler), 15 (Charles O'Rear), 18 (W. Perry Conway), 31 (Nigel J. Dennis; Gallo Images),
36 (Eric and David Hosking), 38 (Galen Rowell), 39 (Clive Druett; Papilio), 44 (D. Robert &
Lorri Franz), 45 (Doug Wechsler), 50 (Macduff Everton), 53 (Karen Tweedy-Holmes), 65
(Theo Allofs), 71 (Layne Kennedy), 72, 78 (Craig Lovell), 79 (Tom Brakefield), 85 (Reuters);
E. R. Degginger/Color-Pic: 35, 69, 83; Phil Degginger/Color-Pic: 90; Digital Vision: 24, 28,
29, 32, 37, 48, 61, 64, 70, 88; Frank Lane Picture Agency/Corbis: 66 (Martin B. Withers), 87
(Terry Whittaker); Wolfgang Kaehler/Corbis: 51, 80; Tom & Pat Leeson: 91; Joe
McDonald/Corbis: 30, 33, 76; Photodisc: 19, 62; Fritz Prenzel/Animals Animals/Earth
Scenes: 9, 22; James P. Rowan: 8; Paul A. Souders/Corbis: 46, 57; David Watts/Tom
Stack & Associates: 21.

[LIBRARY OF CONGRESS CATALOGING-IN-PUBLICATION DATA]
CIP data available

Table of Contents

Chapter One

Defining Grasslands

A black rhinoceros gnaws on tough grasses in Kruger National Park, South Africa. The rhino senses danger. He smells the scent of man in the air. Rhinos have only three enemies: old age, disease, and humans.

▲ A black rhino can charge at speeds up to 30 miles (48 kilometers) per hour.

On this day, two **poachers** are hunting the **endangered** beast. They do not want the hide or the meat. They want only the rhino's horn. The horn is ground up for medicine in Asia or is used to make knife handles in Yemen.

Once, black rhino and white rhino populations were wiped out in Kruger Park. In 1961, scientists reintroduced white rhinos into the **ecosystem.** Black rhinos were added in 1971. Since then, both populations have increased.

Poaching killed many rhinos. Strict laws against poaching have allowed herds to increase. From 1999 to 2001, the total white rhino population grew by 1,265 animals. Black rhinos increased by nearly 400 animals. Still, scientists and park rangers constantly battle poachers to save these magnificent beasts.

What Are Grasslands?

Rhinos are just one of many species that thrive in grasslands. A grassland **biome**

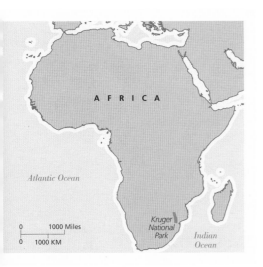

▲ Africa's Kruger National Park

> **? WORDS TO KNOW . . .**
>
> **biome (BYE-ohm)** a large ecosystem in which the plants and animals are adapted to a particular climate or physical environment
>
> **ecosystem (EE-koh-siss-tuhm)** a community of plants and animals and their relationship with the surrounding environment
>
> **endangered (en-DAYN-jurd)** on the edge of being completely wiped out; few members of a species still surviving
>
> **poachers (POHCH-urz)** people who hunt or fish illegally

▲ Scattered white clouds will not bring rain to the dry grasslands of Bushveld Kruger Park, South Africa.

is one in which grass covers most of the land. Grasslands can be tropical or temperate. Tropical grasslands in Africa host many grazing animals. The soil is often poor, and there are distinctly seasonal **precipitation** patterns—wet and dry seasons. Temperate grasslands have few large mammal species, usually fertile soil, and a semiarid climate, which means it receives 10 to 20 inches (25 to 51 centimeters) of precipitation a year. Fire has been important in both types of grasslands. Few trees grow in grasslands, but wildflowers prosper.

Grasslands can form naturally or can be man-made. Glaciers, or huge sheets of ice, paved the way for some grasslands 12,000 years ago. The glaciers flattened the land and plowed down trees. As the glaciers melted, they left behind a flat, open plain. Grass began to grow.

Salt seas once covered other land that today is grassland. As the land rose and the seas disappeared, high plains appeared. Grasses soon covered the plains.

Man-made grasslands, called derived grasslands, result when humans clear forests or fill in wetlands with soil. Usually, the land becomes crop fields. When the soil no longer supports crops, farmers abandon the fields. Wild grasses take over, and grasslands appear.

The Grass

If people allowed their lawns to grow, the grass might reach 2 feet (.61 meters) tall or more. Their lawns would sprout flowers and produce seeds.

In the wild, grasses don't get mowed weekly. They grow to their natural heights, which

> **! WOULD YOU BELIEVE?**
>
> Elephants can also create grasslands. Elephants eat huge amounts of leaves, twigs, and branches. They knock over trees and clear land as efficiently as workers with bulldozers. Within a short time, grass takes over the land cleared by elephants.

> **READ IT!**
>
> Uncover the basics of the grassland biome. Read *Grassland* by Edward R. Ricciuti (Benchmark, 1996).

can reach 10 to 12 feet (3 to 4 m) high. Grasses can be divided into tallgrass and short-grass varieties. Tallgrass species include bamboo, sugarcane, and big bluestem. Short-grass species include buffalo grass and grama. Usually, one or two grass species dominate a grassland region.

Wild grass develops strong, deep root systems. Grass thrives in areas where precipitation measures 10 to 40 inches (25 to 102 cm) yearly. Rainwater soaks into the soil. The roots suck in the water and feed the grass. The roots spread underground, sending up new shoots and leaves. A broad root system helps grass survive fires, grazing animals, freezing weather, and drought.

Tropical Grasslands

Tropical grasslands lie just north and south of the equator. These grasslands,

▲ Only tufts of scrub grasses survive in this Australian grassland.

called savannas, grow in warm to hot climates. They are found in Australia, South America, Africa, and India. Savannas cover nearly half of Africa. The tropical savannas of Africa are ancient and have expanded and contracted with climate changes.

Most experts believe that the North American tallgrass prairie came into being only about 6,000 to 8,000 years ago, after the last glacial period. Origins of the African High Veld—the highest and innermost of South Africa's plateau areas—are unknown. Fire and grazing are believed to have been important to the High Veld's creation.

◄ The short-grass prairie of Theodore Roosevelt National Park in North Dakota is lush and green in the spring.

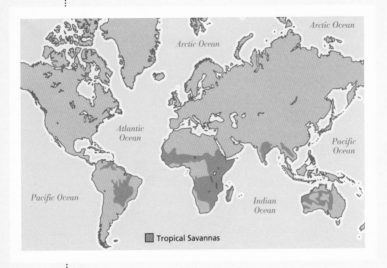

Arctic Ocean

Arctic Ocean

Atlantic Ocean

Pacific Ocean

Pacific Ocean

Indian Ocean

■ Tropical Savannas

▲ The world's tropical savannas

Savannas have two basic seasons: wet and dry. The seasons each last about half the year. The dry season is critical for savannas to survive. During this season, fire from lightning strikes burns the grasses and clears the land. New grass growth comes when the rainy season returns. The constant cycle of rain-drought-burn keeps the land clear of trees. Without the dry season, tropical grasslands would become woodlands and forest.

Africa's tropical grasslands teem with animal life. Australian savannas are home to kangaroos, wallabies, wombats, and bandicoots. South American savannas support rheas, capybara, and maned wolves. The African savannas contain many large animals recognized throughout the world. These include lions, cheetahs, zebras, giraffes, elephants, and wildebeests.

Temperate Grasslands

Temperate climates feature hot summers and cold winters. Temperate grasslands have

LOOK IT UP!

Check out the species that slither, gallop, and trample through the world's grasslands. Visit *http://www.blueplanetbiomes.org* and choose from interesting animal profiles to discover more about these creatures.

▲ North Dakota's Badlands are a mixture of sprawling grasslands and stark hills.

flat land or rolling hills. There are few stands of trees, so wind constantly whips the grassland biome.

Temperate grasslands appear in North America, South America, Europe, Asia, and Africa. On a map, these grasslands lie between the Arctic Circle and the Tropic of Cancer in the Northern Hemisphere. In the Southern Hemisphere, they lie between the Tropic of Capricorn and the Antarctic Circle. Each continent has its own name for temperate grasslands.

Grasslands are called steppes in Russia and range from southeastern Europe into Asian Siberia. Winters are bitter cold, with snow and ice covering the land. The steppes are drier than most other grasslands. Wildlife on the Russian steppes includes saiga

▲ Pampas grass grows beside a brook in Chile, South America.

👁 **WATCH IT!**

Once Europe was covered with grasslands similar to the North American prairies. Discover the remains of Europe's great grasslands in *Wild Europe: Wild Grasslands* [ASIN: 1578071836].

Africa. This grassland has many of the same animals as the savannas. However, the climate is different. The veld has less rain and colder winters.

South American pampas cover the sweeping plains in Argentina and Uruguay. This grassland region has rich, fertile soil and extensive grazing land. Seed-eating birds, such as the double-collared seedeater and the pampas finch, live among bunchgrass and mesquite shrubs of the pampas. The Geoffroy's cat, rhea, mara, guanaco, plains viscacha, and pampas fox are some of the region's rare animals.

North America's grasslands are called prairies. These vast open ranges stretch

antelopes, Corsac foxes, susliks, hawks, buzzards, owls, snakes, and hamsters.

The African veld lies at high elevations in South

from the Rocky Mountains in the west to the Appalachian Mountains in the east. The prairie runs from the plains of Kansas and Nebraska to Alberta, Manitoba, and Saskatchewan, Canada.

There are three basic types of prairie: tallgrass, mixed-grass, and short-grass. Tallgrass prairie lies in the eastern region of the Great Plains. This prairie is best characterized by big bluestem, which can grow 6 to 12 feet (2 to 4 m) high—sometimes growing .5 inches (1.3 cm) a day.

Mixed-grass prairie is a blend of tall and short grasses. The grass lies in two distinct layers. The shorter grass reaches about 1 foot (.3 m)

high. Tall grass grows to 4 feet (1.2 m) or more.

Short-grass prairie lies just to the east of the Rocky Mountains. The mountains prevent heavy rainfall. The grass species are those that thrive with less precipitation, such as buffalo grass and grama.

Short-grass prairies once thundered with the hoofbeats of American bison. Today, pronghorns, deer, and jackrabbits share the short-grass

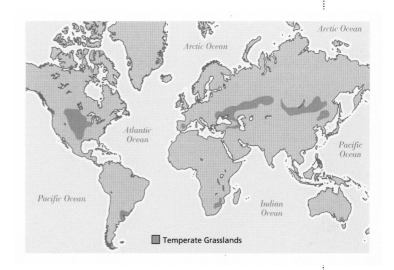

▲ The world's temperate grasslands

prairie with coyotes, badgers, black-footed ferrets, and foxes. Prairie dogs build underground towns beneath the short-grass prairie. There aren't as many prairie dogs as before, but their burrows still serve as homes for prairie rattlesnakes, burrowing owls, and cottontails.

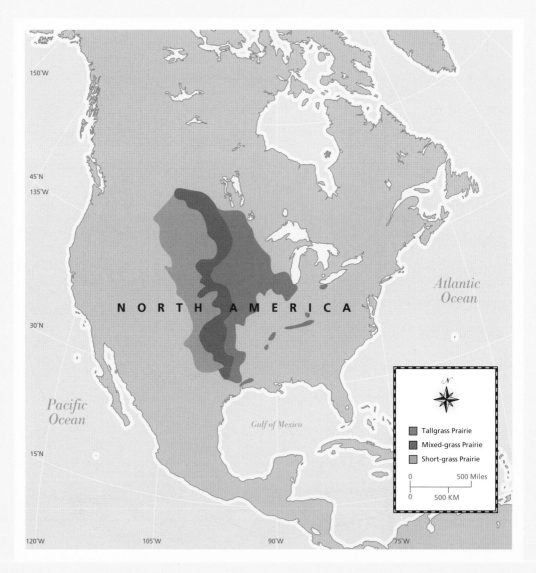

▲ North America's mixed-grass, short-grass, and tallgrass prairies

Chapter Two

Focus on Key Species

A **matriarch** leads her herd deep into the African veld. The female elephant travels paths her ancestors walked hundreds of years ago. She knows where to find water when their current water hole dries up. She has used many water sources over her 56 years.

Her skin bears the scars of a lifetime. She is gray, wrinkled, and huge, weighing in at about 7,000 pounds

> **? WORDS TO KNOW . . .**
>
> **matriarch (MAY-tree-ahrk)** the female leader of a group

▲ Cows and calves form an elephant family unit led by a matriarch.

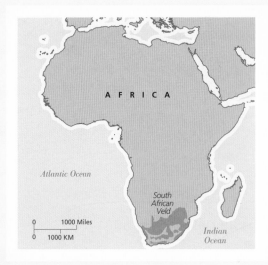

▲ The South African veld

WATCH IT!

Elephants play the starring

role in National Geographic's

Reflections on Elephants

[ASIN: 0792226518].

wary of the elephants' greatest enemy—humans.

Keystone Species

A keystone species is an animal or plant that is crucial for the survival of an ecosystem. The species may change the land or create new habitats. Or, the species may be the main food of area predators. Keystone species of the world's grasslands include elephants, prairie dogs, and other grassland rodents.

(3,175 kilograms). Her right tusk is broken off halfway down. It was damaged in a battle to protect a sickly calf from a pride of lions.

The matriarch is the oldest in this herd of females and their calves. As leader, she must find food and water for the herd. She is constantly aware of predators that might attack calves. And she must be

Elephants are the superspecies of the tropical grasslands of Africa. Elephants build grasslands by clearing forests. They uproot trees, leaving trunks lying on the ground. The trunks support termites, beetles, and other insects. Cleared land allows grass to grow. Grass and its seeds provide nesting material and food for many animals.

Elephant territories extend over grassland and forest regions. Legal protection for elephants covers the herd's vast territory. That means the laws that protect them also cover dozens of other animals and plants living within the elephant's range.

Elephants win popularity contests in every zoo, circus, and wildlife preserve they live in. This popularity

▲ Elephants easily knock over trees on the savanna.

▲ Prairie dogs keep their eyes on possible predators. They chatter to warn of danger.

makes them a flagship species of the grasslands. They draw the attention and action of humans who want to save the species from **extinction.**

Prairie dogs are equally valuable to their ecosystem. Settlers in the short-grass prairie of Canada and the

United States found huge prairie dog towns. They thought the prairie dogs were pests, never realizing how important they were to the prairie's survival.

Prairie dogs dig networks of underground burrows. The digging turns and adds air to the soil. This helps grasses grow. The burrows provide homes for snakes, rodents, black-footed ferrets, and burrowing owls. The prairie dogs feed on grass and seeds. They trim away dead grasses, keeping grass growth healthy. Their **feces** carry plant seeds and spread grassland plants. Finally, hawks, owls, wolves, coyotes, foxes, and black-footed ferrets eat prairie dogs. Dozens of plant and animal species need prairie dogs to survive.

Rodents of all sizes perform services to grassland biomes. Kangaroo rats, pocket gophers, ground squirrels, mice, voles, shrews, moles,

? WORDS TO KNOW . . .

feces (FEE-seez) solid waste of an animal or human

! WOULD YOU BELIEVE?

There were once as many as 5 billion prairie dogs. Humans killed off entire prairie dog towns using poison bait, guns, and traps. Today, prairie dogs live in about 1 percent of the area they covered 200 years ago.

▲ For a coyote, a prairie dog is an ideal dinner.

✋ DO IT!

Create a diagram that shows how several plants and animals are related to one keystone species. Choose prairie dogs or elephants as your keystone species. List all the plants and animals that depend on your keystone species. Place these names in your diagram and show how they are connected.

hamsters, and gerbils are keystone prey. Birds of prey, such as hawks, owls, and falcons, feed on rodents. Rodents are the primary food source for snakes, some lizards, and small predatory cats. Gray wolves can live exclusively on mice and rats. Rodents provide food for dozens of species that could not survive without them.

Umbrella Species

🦎 An umbrella species is a protected animal or plant that spreads its legal protection over other creatures. Governments pass laws to protect endangered or **threatened** species. Hunting, taking land for farming or housing, and building roads put grassland plants and animals at risk. Laws protecting animals or plants with large territories within these ecosystems protect all creatures that live there.

Most people picture Australia as hopping with kangaroos. Two hundred years ago, kangaroo populations were huge. More recently, eastern gray, western gray, and red kangaroo populations have been threatened. The Australian government set up preserves and national parks to save the species. Hunting is forbidden in the preserves. The legal protection that is

This gray kangaroo mother and her joey belong to a larger group, called a mob. ▶

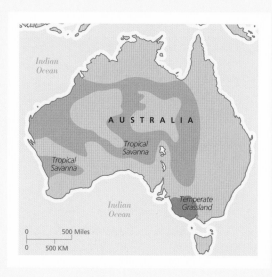

▲ Australia's temperate grasslands and tropical savannas

saving the kangaroos is also saving wallabies, bandicoots, and koalas that live in the kangaroos' natural habitat.

In western North America, the sagebrush prairie supports a number of birds, rodents, lizards, and predators. This region is like

the steppes of Russia—dry, windy, and bitterly cold in the winter. A ground-nesting bird called the sage grouse feeds over a large range in the sagebrush steppes. Protection for this bird would also protect sage sparrows, Brewer's sparrows, sage thrashers, pygmy rabbits, and the sagebrush lizard. Coyotes, wolves, hawks, and owls that prey on these birds would share the umbrella of the sage grouse's protection.

Flagship Species

Flagship species star in nature films, books, and television shows. People are interested in their survival because they are cute, ferocious, or dramatic. In Africa, many endangered species are flagship species.

Three important attention-getters are lions, black rhinos, and white rhinos. Lions are powerful top predators. They have few natural enemies other than humans. Lions have been hunted for sport. During the late 19th and early 20th centuries, many people boasted of their hunting skills by hanging stuffed lion heads on their walls. Extensive hunting and loss of habitat put lions in danger. Rhinos suffer most from poaching. They are killed for their horns.

Organizations support saving lions and rhinos in a number of ways. They write books, shoot films, and sponsor Web sites to educate people about

◄ This long-nosed bandicoot searches for insects and larvae to eat.

▲ Lions are a flagship species of the grasslands.

📖 **READ IT!**

Come face-to-face with the king of the grasslands. Read *The Nature of Lions* by Eric S. Grace (Firefly, 2001).

these species. Government preserves replace lost habitats. People support breeding programs to increase species populations. The efforts to save flagship species also help less-popular species. The hyena and the lion share the same ecosystem. A program that protects lions also protects hyenas.

Indicator Species

Indicator species report on an environment's health. When an indicator species thrives, the ecosystem is healthy. If the species dies or moves away, the ecosystem has problems. In grassland biomes, insects and birds of prey fulfill roles as indicator species.

Butterflies, moths, and other insects that depend on plants help measure the safety of an ecosystem. They move elsewhere or die if food supplies are too low. Their populations increase dramatically when food supplies are high. Insects are easily harmed by pollution. Increases in pollution can be measured by decreases in insect populations.

Swallowtail butterflies flutter over the Russian steppes. They usually lay their eggs on fennel or milk parsley. Swallowtail caterpillars feed on specific plant species: wild carrots, fennel, angelica, and milk parsley. Loss of these plants means loss of swallowtail butterflies. Areas

▲ The Russian steppes in Asia

where land has been taken for farming show a loss of this species.

Birds of prey are top predators in many grassland biomes. They feed on insects, small birds, snakes, lizards, and rodents. They are particularly sensitive to chemical pollution. Poison used to kill rodents or insects, for example, may also destroy populations of owls, hawks, falcons, and eagles.

3

Predators

A Geoffroy's cat twitches its ears, listening for prey. It usually hunts small lizards, insects, and rodents, but it can catch fish and frogs, too.

The cat slips into a river in Argentina's pampas. This cat is a skilled hunter in the water. Today's menu features frogs, which are plentiful in the region.

The size of an average house cat, the Geoffroy's cat is

the most common **feline** predator in temperate South America. The cat weighs about 6 pounds (2.7 kg). Its body measures between 18 and 30 inches (46 and 76 cm) long. The Geoffroy's cat is smaller than its jaguar and panther cousins.

Humans are the cat's only natural enemy. Geoffroy's cats have beautiful coats. Humans hunt the cat for its fur. In 1986, laws banned the sale of Geoffroy's cat fur. Selling the cat as a pet is also against the law.

Top Predators of the Grasslands

Cats are top predators of the grasslands. Lions, cheetahs, jaguars, pumas, leopards, caracals, servals, and Geoffroy's cats hunt in the grasses of different continents. Most grassland cats have fur the color of dry grass. This helps them catch prey because they blend in with their surroundings. Spotted grassland cats such as leopards, servals, and cheetahs have yellow-brown background fur with brown to black spots. They can hide easily in tall grass or shrubs.

▲ South America's pampas

◀ Argentina's Geoffroy's cat will swim after fish and frogs.

The size of a predator usually determines the food it hunts. Large cats need plenty of food and can kill large prey. A pride of hungry lions can succeed against even the largest buffalo. Servals and Geoffroy's cats stick to small prey, such as rodents or birds.

Caracals, on the other hand, do not realize that they are small cats. They'll bring down springboks and even ostriches that weigh two, three, or five times more than the caracals. These cats are known

for leaping into the air to catch flying birds. They can even catch several in one leap!

Grassland canines include small Mexican kit foxes, scrawny coyotes, gray wolves, African hunting dogs, and Australian dingoes. Most canine predators hunt in packs. If they hunt alone, it is usually because they no longer have a pack or because the prey is small and easily caught. Lone canines are most commonly males.

Wolf packs have a specific social organization. The pack leader is called the alpha male. His mate is the alpha female. They are the only wolves in the pack that produce young. When hunting, wolves usually eat according to their rank in

▲ A caracal can jump 6 feet (1.8 m) high to snatch birds out of trees.

the pack. The alpha male eats first, and pups eat last. If there is not enough food, the lower-ranked members of the pack may go hungry.

African hunting dogs prefer hunting impalas and gazelles. These types of antelopes are built for speed—and so are

◀ The coloring on this leopard allows it to hide in tall grass.

African hunting dogs. These wild dogs travel in packs of 20 to 40. The dogs rip the stomachs from animals they catch. The pack feeds in a frenzy, with all members tearing at the body. When young pups are in the pack, they are allowed to eat first. This is the opposite of wolf behavior.

Insectivores

Many predators survive eating mostly insects. It is easy to understand how small birds, meerkats, and lizards can live on these miniature meals. They have small bodies and do not need much food. However, some large animals eat mainly insects, too. They include aardvarks, aardwolves, and rheas.

READ IT!

They're fearless and ferocious. Read about Africa's cats and canines in *African Predators* by Gus Mills and Martin Harvey (Smithsonian, 2001).

▲ The aardvark limits its diet to ants and termites, but there are billions of those insects in African grasslands.

Aardvarks, also called anteaters, feed on ants and termites in the African grasslands. They weigh up to about 140 pounds (64 kg). Aardvarks have long, narrow snouts that are designed for sticking in anthills and termite mounds. Long tongues and gluey saliva help aardvarks collect their meals.

Aardwolves are related to hyenas, but they eat mostly termites. And not just any termite will do. They prefer snouted harvester termites, though they will eat others in a pinch. These termites feed on grasses at night. Aardwolves wait for dark, then lick up the termites

◀ African hunting dogs bring down a wildebeest calf.

by the thousands. One aardwolf may eat a quarter of a million termites in one feeding.

Grassland Reptiles

Every grassland biome has its share of reptiles. There are snakes, lizards, geckos, and tortoises. Most grassland snakes are harmless, such as garter snakes and grass snakes. Several poisonous snakes do make their homes in grasslands. These include black mambas and puff adders in Africa, and rattlesnakes in North America.

Black mambas slither through the central African savannas. They move quickly and are highly dangerous. Black mambas have been known to travel at speeds up to 10 miles (16 km) per hour. Black mamba venom attacks the nervous system.

◀ A red-billed oxpecker cleans insects off a kudu.

▲ A black mamba is coiled and ready to attack. Its venom is deadly to humans and animals.

The venom paralyzes its victims, and they cannot breathe. Mambas usually eat rodents, bats, lizards, and ground-nesting birds.

Rattlesnakes are the only poisonous snakes on the North American prairies. Prairie rattlers are about 3 feet (.9 m) long and are yellow-brown in color. Western diamondbacks are larger—nearly 6 feet (1.8 m) long—and are common in

 READ IT!

An American Safari: Adventures on the North American Prairie by Jim Brandenburg (Walker & Co., 1995) takes readers on a trip through rattlesnake country.

▲ The diamondback rattler announces an attack by shaking its rattle.

🤚 **DO IT!**

What can you do to save the environment? Choose a conservation group near you and get involved. Access the Kids Ecology Corps at *http://www. kidsecology.org* to find a group that interests you.

southwestern grasslands. The western rattlesnake enjoys the mountains and grasslands of the western United States, Mexico, and Canada. Its coloring differs, depending on where it lives. In the Sierra Nevada range of the United States, it is nearly black in color with a banded tail. Rattlesnakes feed on rodents, lizards, and ground-nesting birds. The prairie rattler lives in old prairie dog burrows.

The open grasslands are good hunting grounds for birds of prey like this peregrine falcon. ▶

Birds of Prey

 Birds of prey live well in the open grasslands. There are fewer places for prey to hide and more prey available. Birds of prey include those that catch and eat live prey and those that eat **carrion.**

Birds of prey in North America's grasslands include

PROFILE: SWAINSON'S HAWK

Swainson's hawk is a bird of prey that migrates between North American prairies and the Argentinean pampas. Unfortunately, the hawk travels to a place in the pampas where pest-killing chemicals were once heavily used. It feeds on grasshoppers, which have been eating crops sprayed with strong chemicals. The insects that Swainson's hawks have been eating have indirectly poisoned the birds. To save the Swainson's hawks from extinction, the government of Argentina has banned the use of certain pest killers.

> **? WORDS TO KNOW . . .**
>
> carrion (CAH-ree-uhn) dead or rotting flesh

PROFILE: SAKER FALCONS

Saker falcons live on the plains and steppes of Europe and Asia. They are large falcons, standing about 18 inches (46 cm) tall. Saker falcons specialize in hunting rodents. Their excellent eyesight allows them to fly high above the steppes, then dive down to catch their food. Estimates show that about 1,000 breeding pairs live on the Russian steppes, and another 130 pairs live in Europe. Humans are the main danger for saker falcons. These birds are caught and trained for a form of sport hunting called falconry.

burrowing owls, peregrine falcons, eagles, and hawks. Burrowing owls live on the short-grass prairie in prairie dog burrows. The owls can dig their own homes but are content to take over empty burrow space. They eat crickets, grasshoppers, beetles, young prairie dogs, and small lizards. Peregrine falcons feed on birds. They catch their prey in flight. Peregrine falcons are the world's fastest birds. They can dive at a rate of more than 200 miles (322 km) per hour.

In Africa, secretary birds do not catch prey in flight. Instead, they catch food while walking through the savanna. Secretary birds feed on rodents, mammals, other birds, insects, and snakes.

▲ Secretary birds catch their prey by walking through the grasslands and picking up insects, ground,birds, and eggs.

Their skill in catching and killing snakes is remarkable. When they find a snake, they flutter their wings, then run around wildly. Thoroughly confused, the snake stops moving, and the secretary bird pounces. These birds kill poisonous snakes by pounding the snakes' heads on rocks.

Carrion feeders find plenty of food on the grasslands. They eat leftover rot-ting flesh. The meat may be the remains of a lion's or puma's catch. Or it may be from an animal dying from injury or age. Buzzards, vultures, and marabou storks are carrion eaters. They are grassland garbage disposals.

Successful Predators

🦎 Not every hunt results in catching prey. Species that hunt large Cape buffaloes or

▲ A patient lioness stalks zebra in this Kenya grassland.

zebras may make a catch only once in 4, 10, or even 20 tries. Those that hunt insects, however, eat daily. There is much more insect prey available, and it is easier to catch.

Predators fulfill an important role in nature. They keep prey populations from exploding. Rodents and birds keep insects from taking over grasslands. Hawks, owls, and snakes control rodent populations. Every predator has its part to play in keeping nature's balance.

Chapter Four

Prey

A Corsac fox emerges from its burrow in the steppes of Turkestan. It smells a bobak marmot, a type of rodent, near-by. The marmot knows the fox is close but is not too worried.

Corsac foxes need help when hunting. Unlike most foxes, they may hunt in packs. Their hearing and sense of smell are excellent, which helps

▲ Corsac foxes move too slowly to catch rodents. Usually, they end up eating seeds, berries, and insects.

▲ Asia's Turkestani steppes

Supply and Demand

🐇 Grasslands have many creatures that serve as prey for hungry animals. These include insects, reptiles, amphibians, rodents, and ground-nesting birds. These animal groups provide the most prey in other land biomes as well.

Savannas have three major insect groups: ants, termites, and grasshoppers and locusts. These are not the only insects on the savanna, just the ones with the largest populations. Prairies and steppes also have grasshoppers and locusts, along with beetles, wasps, weevils, flies, and hundreds of other insect species. As is true with other land biomes, the insect population is, by far, the largest.

them locate prey. But catching the prey is another story. Corsac foxes are so slow that they cannot even outrun a lazy dog.

The fox gets too close, and the marmot skitters away. It is a good thing for the Corsac fox that it eats both meat and plants. Today's hunt failed, and the fox must feed on insects, seeds, and berries instead.

👁 **WATCH IT!**

Discover the mysteries within the insect world. Check out *Eyewitness: Insects* [ASIN: 6303863449].

▲ This massive termite mound houses millions of termite workers and their queen.

Ants and termites live in colonies with populations in the thousands. Individually, an ant or termite is not much of a meal. In a colony, they become a feast. Birds, lizards, toads, geckos, anteaters, aard-wolves, and echidnas feed on ants and termites.

Termite mounds are highly visible in tropical grasslands. They usually rise up to 10 feet (3 m) above the ground. Within the mound, the colony works to feed and

> **(!) WOULD YOU BELIEVE?**
>
> Termites in Australia built a mound 20 feet (6 m) high. The base measured 30 feet (9 m) across. Mounds are made from soil, saliva, and feces. The mixture dries as hard as rock.

protect the queen and king. The queen and king are sealed into a chamber where they mate to produce more termites. One queen can produce up to 30,000 eggs a day. The eggs are placed in chambers where they will hatch. Soldier termites protect the nest from predators.

Grasshoppers and locusts feed other insects, lizards, snakes, mammals, and birds. But the grasshoppers and locusts don't care whether their own food is wild grass or farm crops. Huge numbers of grasshoppers or locusts can destroy acres of crops in a few hours. A swarm of locusts or grasshoppers attacks grasslands and farmlands somewhere in the world

▲ A black racer slithers through a short-grass prairie.

every year. These attacks are called plagues.

Larger Prey

🦎 **Carnivores** get all their nutrition from eating meat. They do not need to eat a balanced diet like humans. Meat and water fulfill all their needs.

Grassland reptiles live in burrows underground or in shrubs or thick clumps of grass. Hundreds of harm-less lizards, skinks, geckos, and snakes prosper in grass-lands. They prey on insects and small rodents, and serve as food for dozens of larger animals.

Tropical savannas produce an abundance of seeds and grasses for hungry birds. Many seed-eating birds feed on the ground. While feeding, these birds are open to attack from predators. Lizards and snakes

> ? **WORDS TO KNOW . . .**
>
> **carnivores (KAR-nuh-vorz)**
>
> animals that eat meat

have little trouble catching ground-feeding birds.

On North American prairies, the greater prairie chicken was once common, but its population is declining. Prairie chickens make good eating for hawks, owls, and other prairie hunters.

Rats for Dinner

Kangaroo rats, harvest mice, and prairie dogs are all grassland rodents. They come in sizes ranging from a couple of ounces up to several pounds. Carnivorous mammals, large reptiles, and birds of prey hunt rodents, as well as small mammals such as shrews and moles.

Black-tailed prairie dogs are a primary food for black-footed ferrets, coyotes, wolves, owls, and hawks. The prairie dogs keep watch for predators. They stick their heads above their holes and bark when danger comes close.

Rabbits and hares also serve as grassland prey. Jackrabbits are a popular

◀ Greater prairie chickens are ground birds that nest in tufts of grass.

▲ Black-tailed prairie dogs once numbered in the millions on North America's Great Plains.

menu item for coyotes, gray wolves, and great horned owls. In North American grasslands, predators control rabbit populations.

The rabbit situation is a different story in Australia. Rabbits were originally brought from England but have no natural enemies in Australia. Within a short time, the rabbit population exploded. Rabbits eat grasses and shrubs, as well as crops. Australian ranchers and farmers put up rabbit fences to keep hordes of them from invading grazing land.

Defensive Measures

🦎 Many types of prey have some means of protecting themselves from predators. In grassland ecosystems, **camouflage** is important. Many species have skin or fur the color of grass. Tall grasses even hide zebras with their vivid black-and-white stripes. Most animals see only in black and white. A zebra's stripes look just like waving grasses to the average predator.

Living underground is another means of defense. Prairie dogs, kit foxes, rodents, rabbits, and reptiles have protected underground burrows. Many burrows have several exits. If a predator starts to dig at the front door, the prey scoots out the back.

Prey also protect themselves by looking for food at night. Under cover of

◀ Fenced grassland prevents the normal movement of animals across the land.

▲ A herd of zebra grazes on the Etosha Plain in Namibia, Africa.

darkness, prey can slip, slither, and skitter through dry, rattling grasses without being seen. However, predators do not all rely on eyesight for catching their prey. Snakes use temperature sensors to detect the location of warm-blooded animals. Foxes, wolves, and coyotes have excellent senses of smell and hearing. Owls, which do depend on sight,

▲ Giraffes are the tallest grassland species. Their height lets them feed off treetop leaves.

have outstanding night vision. They can see rodents and rabbits even in the dark.

Every Animal Becomes Prey

🦎 Alive or dead, every grassland animal feeds others. Prey may be the eggs, infants, or adults of a species. It can also be the carrion left when animals die. Even the largest grassland beasts—elephants, rhinos, and giraffes—eventually die and feed insects, rodents, and vultures.

The eaters and the eaten create an intricate web. Small insects feed on plants, other insects, or the flesh of dead animals. They feed larger insects, birds, amphibians, reptiles, and mammals. The cycle of eating and being eaten extends to the largest beasts. All plants and animals supply food to some creature. It is the way nature maintains its balance.

Chapter Five

Flora

A male mountain plover attracts a mate on the short-grass prairie of Montana. The two build their nest amid scruffy buffalo grass. The plover eggs—olive green speckled with black—will blend in well with the grasses.

The region is dotted with prairie dog holes. The prairie dogs feed on buffalo grass. They constantly "mow" the areas around their holes. Their actions keep buffalo grass and blue grama healthy.

The plovers share their grassy territory with local cattle, deer, pronghorns, rabbits, and prairie dogs. These

▲ A mountain plover looks for a mate amid the buffalo grass.

species depend on buffalo grass and blue grama for food. Spring thaws bring fresh

▲ North America's short-grass prairies

shoots to munch on. In summer, pale yellow and golden flowers dance on stalks above the blades of grass. By fall, the grass clusters have turned a delicate lavender. Throughout the seasons, grasses feed and shelter countless animals.

Grasses

Grasses have thick, dense root systems and shoots that rise above the ground. They

▲ An Indian rhino plows a path through tall elephant grass.

produce flowers to make seeds. Grasses—natural or human-seeded—belong to several groups: grazing grasses, ornamental grasses, cereal, sugarcane, and woody grasses.

Natural grasses that grow in savannas, steppes, and prairies are usually grazing grasses. These grasses may be short, such as buffalo grass and blue grama. Short grasses usually do not grow taller than 2 feet (.61 m). Tall grasses, such as big bluestem, Sudan grass, and elephant grass, grow to heights of 6 to 10 feet (1.8 to 3 m).

Showy grasses grow naturally in savannas. Pampas grass, for example, is a thick cluster of grass with tall stems.

◂ Sagebrush and wild grasses cover this Montana prairie.

▲ Tall, sturdy bamboo is a woody type of grass.

Long before humans began planting grain crops, nature produced cereals. Wild forms of barley, oats, corn, and wheat grew in grasslands. Foxtail barley, side-oats grama, and western wheatgrass are three naturally growing grassland grains.

Sugarcane is another crop grass grown for sale. However, sugarcane also grows naturally in many tropical grasslands. Sugarcane reaches up to 15 feet (4.6 m) tall. The main stem is thick and is filled with raw sugar.

Woody grasses are types of bamboo. The stems can be quite thick—nearly 1 foot (.3 m) across. Bamboo is common in Asian grasslands. Some types of bamboo have

Pampas grass flowers look like soft beige feathers. Many people plant pampas grass in North American gardens, but this grass grows naturally in Argentina and Uruguay.

been known to grow as tall as 120 feet (37 m), although this is unusual.

Forbs

🦎 Few people know what a *forb* is, although they see forbs every day. A forb is any low plant that grows in grasslands but is not grass. Wildflowers such as daisies, black-eyed Susans, and prairie coneflowers are forbs. Stinging nettles, sagebrush, and tumbleweeds are also forbs.

Wildflowers brighten up the springtime prairie. They range in color from the milk-white of prairie fringed orchids to the bright yellow of evening primrose. Delicate lavender spiderwort and pink fame-flower wave above blue grama.

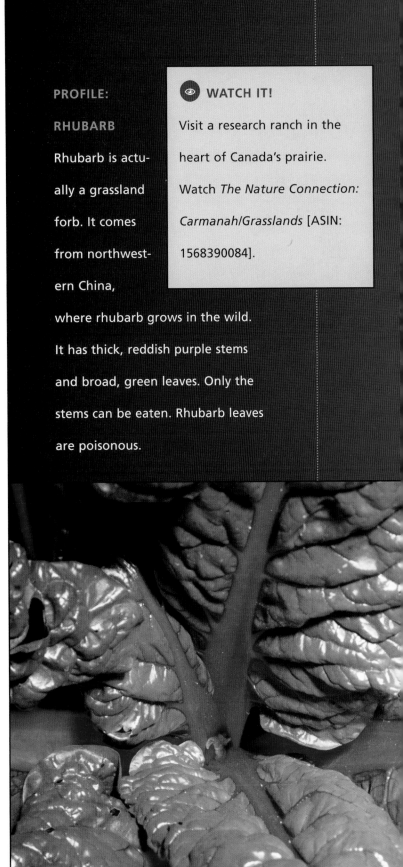

PROFILE:

RHUBARB

Rhubarb is actu-
ally a grassland
forb. It comes
from northwest-
ern China,
where rhubarb grows in the wild.
It has thick, reddish purple stems
and broad, green leaves. Only the
stems can be eaten. Rhubarb leaves
are poisonous.

👁 **WATCH IT!**

Visit a research ranch in the
heart of Canada's prairie.
Watch *The Nature Connection:
Carmanah/Grasslands* [ASIN:
1568390084].

▲ Tickseed sunflowers paint the prairie bright yellow.

🖱 **LOOK IT UP!**

The United States Geological Survey offers plenty of information about prairie wildflowers at *http://www.npwrc.usgs.gov/resource/literatr/wildflwr/wildflwr.htm.*

Many grassland wildflowers were used by Native Americans to make herbal medicines. Coneflower, also called echinacea, treated acne, bee stings, and snake bites. Tea from sunflower leaves relieved lung diseases. Pennyroyal tea treated headaches and mouth sores.

Tumbleweed brings to mind western movies with cowboys and cattle herds. However, this forb is actually an immigrant from Mongolia.

Its common name is Russian thistle. Tumbleweed grows in dry plains. The reason it tumbles is simple—that is how it spreads seeds. When a tumbleweed plant produces seeds, the plant breaks off at the base. The round bush rolls along the ground and drops its seeds.

Sagebrush is another common grassland shrub. It is found on the Russian steppes, Mongolian steppes, and in the Great Plains. Sagebrush is an excellent grazing plant. It is rich in protein, so it provides good nutrition for cattle.

Trees Amid the Grasses

Trees in the grasslands are few, but important. They provide shade for hot creatures, nesting for birds, and strong roots to hold down soil. The most common tree in the African savannas is the acacia (uh-CAY-shuh). There are many varieties of acacia, including whistling thorn trees and gum acacias. Acacias have small leaves and tiny flowers. They make excellent eating. Elephants, antelopes, and giraffes all feed on their leaves.

Africa's baobab (BAY-o-bab) is a tree of which legends are told. According to an Arabian tale, the devil pulled a baobab tree out of the ground. He turned it over and stuck the tree back in the ground with it roots hanging in the air. The legend explains why a

! WOULD YOU BELIEVE?

Gum from the Senegal gum acacia is used to make face cream, eyewash, and medicine for diarrhea. It also is used to flavor soft drinks.

55

PROFILE: WHISTLING THORNS AND ANTS

Whistling thorn acacias grow on the African savannas. The tree grows sharp, 3-inch (7.6-cm) thorns with round bases. The trees are home to nigriceps ants. The ants drill small holes into the thorns to build their nests. When the wind blows, flutelike music whistles through the thorns.

The ants protect their home against all visitors—other insects, birds, and giraffes. Without the ants, the whistling thorn trees would be eaten. The ants deliver a painful sting. If a giraffe decides to munch on the acacia's leaves, the ants swarm out of their nests. They attack the giraffe, stinging its snout and tongue.

baobab stands leafless for three-quarters of the year—its branches are supposed to be its roots! This tree grows so large that people can live in the trunks.

Australia has hundreds of varieties of eucalyptus. Some have round leaves and others have spear-shaped leaves. The tree's oil is used to make medicines for coughs, colds, and sore throats. North Americans often use eucalyptus oil in cough drops and chest rubs.

Prairies and steppes have different trees than savannas. Lower rates of precipitation, strong winds, and cold winters require hardier trees than those that grow in African and South American savannas. The cold and wind keep trees

▲ Eucalyptus trees flourish on Australia's grasslands.

from growing very tall on the prairie.

Common trees on the North American prairie include willows, elms, oaks, and cottonwoods. Prairie trees stand alone or in small clusters. The southern plains of Kansas and Nebraska support a number of fruit trees. Persimmons, Osage orange (which is really a type

▲ Russian olive trees are scattered across the steppes.

of mulberry), big tree plum, black cherry, and crab-apple grow well in dry prairie environments.

Russian steppes support different species of trees than North American prairies do. The Russian olive tree is a common steppe tree. It survives bitterly cold winters and low rainfall rates.

Russian steppes have many low-lying bushes that grow in clusters like short, stunted forests. The shrubs include thorn, pear, plum, and hawthorn bushes. In some places, juniper trees invade natural grasslands. They compete with Russian thistle (a tumbleweed) and wild thyme for growing room.

Chapter Six

Herbivores

🐇 A pair of maras munch on the sparse grasses of the Patagonian grasslands in South America. The two rodents are lifelong mates. This is odd for rodents. Few rodent species choose a mate for any longer than it takes to produce young.

The maras have a strange appearance. Their bodies are shaped like rabbits, but they have long, thin legs. They hop and leap like rabbits, too. Their faces more closely resemble kangaroos than rabbits.

▲ Maras, like this one in Patagonia, South America, can live in colonies of up to 15 pairs.

▲ South America's Patagonian grasslands

The maras live in a colony of about 15 pairs and their young. They all share a den, but each family keeps a feeding territory to itself. Males protect these feeding territories from invaders, even if the invader is another mara that shares the den.

Maras can weigh up to 35 pounds (16 kg) and are too large for small predators to

handle. Still, the mara population is declining. European brown hares have invaded mara feeding ranges. The mara's natural habitat cannot support two similar species. The hares are eating the maras out of their home.

Large Plant Eaters

The largest grassland animals are plant eaters. In Africa and Asia, these include elephants, rhinos, hippos, and Cape or water buffaloes. In North America, large plant eaters include pronghorns, elk, and bison. Australia's largest **herbivores** are brumbies (wild horses), wild camels, and kangaroos.

Elephants can eat up to 500 pounds (227 kg) of plant

> **?** WORDS TO KNOW . . .
>
> herbivores (HUR-buh-vorz)
>
> animals that eat plants

▲ These Cape buffaloes in Tanzania, Africa, fend off lion attacks with their massive horns.

matter a day. This includes grasses, leaves, shrubs, and tree branches. To have an ample food supply, elephant herds travel over a wide territory.

African, or Cape, buffaloes are fearsome and fearless. They have massive horns that they use to fend off predators. Cape buffaloes travel in herds that also provide protection. When attacked, the herd forms a defensive circle. Even lions dare not

? WORDS TO KNOW ...

ungulates (UHNG-gyoo-luhts)

mammals with hoofs

attack a healthy adult buffalo herd. Buffaloes graze on grasses and leaves.

Where the Deer and the Antelope Roam

Deer, antelopes, wilde- beests, and warthogs are **ungulates.** Some species have horns, such as Cape buf- faloes. Some ungulates, such as wildebeests and plains zebras, travel in herds. Others, such as mule deer, prefer living alone.

▲ Overhunting and habitat loss have reduced the blackbuck population on India's plains from 4 million to about 10,000.

All ungulates are herbivores. They feed on grasses and leaves. Most cover a large feeding territory. They move on a schedule, meaning the herds are in a specific area at the same time each year.

The Russian steppes support a most unusual ungulate—the saiga antelope. The saiga is a small antelope with a snout like a short trunk. Saigas travel in small herds of 30 to 40 animals. A normal herd includes a buck (male), his harem of does (females), and young. Males have long, amber horns that they use to protect their harem.

On the North American prairies, pronghorns once had a population of nearly

PROFILE: WARTHOGS

The fierce-looking warthog is an herbivore that feeds on grasses, bulbs, and roots. Warthogs get their name from the four large mounds, or warts, on their faces. A warthog's tusks are used to protect its family, called a sounder, from predators. Angry males will chase away lions, leopards, and African hunting dogs to keep their sounders safe.

▲ White rhinos have been hunted nearly to extinction by poachers who kill the animals for their horns.

? WORDS TO KNOW . . .

marsupials (mahr-SOO-pee-uhlz) order of animals in which the young develop in pouches on the mother's body

tion numbered about 20,000 pronghorns. Hunting limits allowed the species to recover. Today, nearly 1 million pronghorns live in North America.

Hunters have killed animals by the millions for their horns, tusks, and antlers. Records show that traders sold 350,000 pairs of saiga horns between 1840 and 1850. Tibetan antelopes and both black and white rhinos have been hunted nearly to extinction for their horns. Elephant poaching forced a worldwide ban on the sale of ivory to save the species.

Marsupials

Although there are **marsupials** on several continents,

35 million animals. The pronghorns were hunted extensively from the time Europeans arrived in the West. By the 1920s, the popula-

the greatest number live in Australia. Marsupials include kangaroos and wallabies. These animals live on the Australian savanna.

Kangaroos were once plentiful across the continent. As settlers tried to tame the savanna and establish sheep and cattle ranches, kangaroos lost territory. Fences could not keep the leaping kangaroos from water or healthy grass. Instead, ranchers killed kangaroos to preserve grass for cows and sheep. Wallabies have been less of a problem. They are about one-fourth the size of red kangaroos and cannot hop over fences as easily. Both species suffer from loss of habitat and overgrazing by sheep and cattle.

▲ Rock wallabies look much like short kangaroos. This mother carries a joey in her pouch.

Leaves, Berries, and Seeds

Seed-eating birds include a range of songbirds and game birds. Various species of quail, pigeons, and finches can be

found on grasslands throughout the world. Australian
grasslands add some remarkably colorful birds to their
seed-eating list: rosellas,
parrots, and sulfur-
crested cockatoos.

Ostriches, rheas, and
emus are large flightless
birds. Their bodies weigh
so much that their wings
can't lift them. A full-sized
male ostrich can weigh
more than 300 pounds

📖 **READ IT!**

Learn more about seed-eating
birds. Read *Birds: National
Audubon Society First Field
Guides* by Scott Weidensaul
(Scholastic, 1998).

(136 kg). Ostriches live in African savannas. Rheas are the ostriches of the South American pampas. They weigh about 50 pounds (23 kg) and live in flocks of 5 to 30 birds. Emus live exclusively in Australia. They weigh between 65 and 100 pounds (29 and 45 kg). All these birds eat grasses, seeds, leaves, and fruit. Ostriches also munch on grasshoppers and locusts. Rheas add insects and lizards to their diets, while emus will eat mice and lizards.

Rodents of all sizes munch their way through the world's grasslands. Gerbils, prairie dogs, hamsters, kangaroo rats, and field mice find plenty to eat from grass seeds, berries, and leaves. Even bitterly cold Mongolia has a tiny gerbil that survives on roots and seeds.

Herbivores help spread plants in grasslands and keep them healthy. Burrow diggers turn over and refresh soil. Grass eaters

! **WOULD YOU BELIEVE?**

Rheas have very odd nesting habits. A male rhea builds a grass-lined nest. Then he attracts as many females as he can to his nest. Each female lays one egg. A clutch of rhea eggs has up to 30 eggs—from 30 different mothers. The male sits on the eggs until they hatch. He feeds and raises the young by himself.

▲ The Mongolian grasslands in Asia

◂ Australia's crimson rosellas feed on seeds in Queensland grasslands.

▲ This tiny kangaroo rat would fit in the palm of your hand.

DO IT!

Become part of the effort to save black-tailed prairie dogs. Find out what you can do at *http://www.prairiedogs.org.*

chew away old growth and encourage new sprouts. Herbivores eat large quantities of seeds. They spread seeds through their solid waste. Plant eaters and plants need each other to survive. Without the plants, there would be no food for plant eaters. Without plant eaters, new growth would become rare, as old growth would choke the life from prairies and savannas.

A Cycle of Life

🐾 Fingers of white lightning cut across the black night sky. Thunder rumbles over the savanna seconds later. Skittish zebras twitch their muscles. They will bolt at the first sign of danger. A vast herd of wildebeests huddles together. A male lion roars in the darkness. Grassland animals are nervous tonight.

The end of the dry season is coming . . . but not yet.

▲ Lightning streaks across a stormy sky in Tanzania.

▲ Wildfire spreads through grasslands, sending animals fleeing for their lives.

Tonight's lightning brings no rain. Toward dawn, a lightning strike sets savanna grasses on fire. Winds from the east blow across the plain, pushing the fire onward.

Springboks rush to avoid the fast-moving flames. Zebras and wildebeests are on the run. Lions pass up the chance for an easy kill. They, too, head for safety. Burrowing lizards, snakes, and rodents huddle down in their holes. The fire should sweep over

▲ The world's tropical grasslands

Tropical Grasslands

Arctic Ocean

Arctic Ocean

Atlantic Ocean

Pacific Ocean

Pacific Ocean

Indian Ocean

their homes quickly. They'll be safe underground.

Birds of prey hover in the smoky air at the fire's edge. They know that wildfires create a banquet for the taking. They swoop down to snag panicky animals fleeing the flames.

After devouring all the grass within view, the fire quickly burns itself out. The savanna lies in ashes, blackened and bare. The air carries a scent of burning. And yet, this fire is as much a part of the savanna cycle of life as rain and sun.

Life-Giving Fire

Fire plays a key role in the survival of grassland biomes. It clears dead grass and shrubs.

It removes trees from the savanna. And it feeds the soil.

Dead grass and shrubs can become so thick on the savanna that

Burned tree stumps serve as a reminder that a brushfire passed this way.

DO IT!

Fires started by nature or controlled by rangers are necessary. Fires started by careless campers are not. They can be destructive. When you camp in a grassland region, douse your campfire. Make sure all coals are out. Never light fires during a drought or fire ban. Never leave a fire unattended.

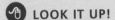 **LOOK IT UP!**

Learn about what scientists do at an Arizona-based research ranch to protect our bioregions and ecosystems. Visit *http://www.audubon.org/local/sanctuary/appleton/*.

nothing new can grow. Without fire, the grasslands die. Fires "weed" out the old to make room for the new.

Surprisingly, many seeds rely on fire to bring them to life. The heat burns away or bursts seed coverings. When rains come, these seeds send down roots and begin to grow.

Trees threaten the grassland ecosystem. A few scattered trees are important, but a forest of trees kills the grasslands. Young trees do not survive wildfires. They are also "weeded" out.

Some trees actually thrive because of fire. A fire clears out competing shrubs, bushes, and young trees. Larger trees survive fires because they have thick, fire-resistant bark. They

◄ Thick trees like this baobab in Botswana stand a better chance of surviving fire.

keep enough water in their roots and branches to withstand the fire's heat.

After a fire, ashes cover the soil. The ashes contain chemicals that feed the soil. The chemicals are **nutrients** that nature uses as a fertilizer. Without fire, these nutrients would not be available. Fires allow the earth to regain a healthy, fertile chemical balance.

Fire and Wildlife

Very little wildlife dies in grass fires. Birds fly away. Mammals run away. Burrowing animals hide underground. Usually, wildlife deaths are limited to grasshoppers, locusts, stick insects, small rodents,

BUSHFIRE IN THE NEWS

After nearly a decade of drought, Australia's grasslands are like fields of kindling—one spark and the grasses will burst into flames. The government has tried using fire to fight fire. Rangers light controlled fires to reduce the amount of "fuel" lying in the grasslands. The controlled fires build firebreaks, which are areas cleared of vegetation, that stop wildfires from spreading.

Bushfires cover huge areas. One rancher fought a bushfire on his property for months. His land was part of more than 1 million acres (405,000 hectares) that was left in ashes from that fire.

> **? WORDS TO KNOW . . .**
>
> nutrients (NOO-tree-uhnts) substances needed by plants, animals, or humans for growth; key elements of food

73

▲ Rain finally comes, bringing new life to the savanna.

and lizards. Dozens of animals feed on the bodies of those killed.

Scientists have found that after a major burn, most animal life increases. Birds fare remarkably well. That's because plants naturally produce more seeds after a fire. It is nature's way of making sure plant species survive. The added seeds attract birds to nest in the area and feed many songbirds and waterfowl. Mourning doves, larks, grouse, and sparrows show population increases after a grass fire.

Mammals return to burned areas quickly. Once the rains come, new grasses and wildflowers provide excellent grazing. Herbi-

vores, such as antelopes, zebras, and wildebeests, graze on new grass growth.

When the Rains Come

Within weeks of the burning season, rain comes to the savanna. Ashes on the land mix with water and sink into the soil. They feed the seeds and roots beneath the surface. New plants sprout. Tall grasses can grow as much as 1 or 2 inches (2.5 or 5 cm) in a day. Wildflowers bloom and bring color back to the plains.

Because so much food becomes available, animal species produce more young. Eventually, an area that was blackened and barren of life prospers.

8

The Serengeti National Park

✍ A wildebeest cow delivers her calf on the grassy plains of the Serengeti. It is June, and hundreds of thousands of calves are born within a few weeks. A newborn struggles to rise on wobbly legs. Although it seems impossible, the unsteady calf will be able to run with its herd within a few days of its birth.

It is time for the great migration. About 2 million wildebeest and 200,000

zebras will follow the rains in search of fresh grass. They will take the same routes their ancestors followed more than 2,000 years ago.

It is a trip filled with dangers. The herd begins its migration at a slow walk. Soon, the urge to move takes hold. The herd is now on the run. Thousands will die on this trip. Old wildebeests will drop behind and become the prey of lions, leopards, and hyenas. Young calves will drown as their parents race across fast-flowing rivers. Stampeding beasts will trample the bodies of those that fall. Even the healthiest may become meals for the crocodiles that inhabit Serengeti rivers.

▲ Serengeti National Park in Africa

The Park

 The Serengeti National Park was founded in 1913. The name *Serengeti* comes from the Maasai word that means "the place where the land moves on forever." The park is the result of a regional effort to preserve and protect the natural treasures of Kenya and Tanzania.

> 📖 **READ IT!**
>
> Each year, millions of wildebeest travel well-worn paths through the Serengeti Plain. Follow their trek in Jonathan Scott's *The Great Migration* (Rodale, 1989).

◄ Wildebeest migrate across a river on the Serengeti Plain.

▲ Lions relax in the safety of the Serengeti National Park.

👁 **WATCH IT!**

Go on safari to Africa's

magnificent Serengeti Plain.

Watch *Africa: The Serengeti*

[ASIN: B00004REBF].

Serengeti supports many of the strangest, largest, most endangered, and most fascinating animals on earth. It is home to what park officials call the Big Five—the animals most visitors want to see: elephants, lions, leopards, rhinos, and Cape buffaloes.

Flagship Species

🦎 When organizations are looking for flagship species to promote conservation, they need look no further than the Serengeti National Park. On this African savanna, elephants lumber in neat lines through the tall grasses. Giraffes stretch to feed on acacia leaves. Leopards stalk skittish antelopes in hope of a meal. Nearsighted rhinos charge through the brush, then forget what they are chasing. The roars of lions echo across the land.

Rivers and water holes attract Cape buffaloes. These massive creatures rarely go far from water. They prefer to spend their days lying in mud. By doing this, however, they face a distinct danger from the 15-foot (4.6-m)-long Nile crocodiles.

Herds of wildebeests and antelopes graze on the open plains. Vividly striped zebras blend in with the waving grass as they graze. They all keep a wary eye out for predators. Klipspringers and

LOOK IT UP!

The Serengeti Plain supports animals, plants, and people. Visit *http://www.serengeti.org* and discover the beauty of this African wilderness.

▲ A leopard stalks its prey, hoping to find a careless antelope near a water hole.

▲ The rhinoceros beetle gets its name from the horns on its head.

dik-diks jump about through the tall grass.

Big Names, Small Critters

A number of small Serengeti creatures have big names to live up to. They are ant lions, rhinoceros beetles, elephant shrews, and buffalo weavers.

Ant lions are serious predators that build traps for their victims. As larvae, ant lions capture ants and crawling insects in a round pit. As the prey try to escape, the movement alerts the ant lion larvae. The larvae emerge from the sand and gobble down their dinner.

Rhinoceros beetles are the world's strongest animals. Yes, elephants move more bulk because of their sheer size, but they can carry only about one-fourth of their own weight. These beetles can carry 850 times their own weight.

Among shrews, which are usually quite small, the elephant shrew is a giant. It can weigh up to 1.5 pounds (680 grams) and measures close to 1 foot long (.3 m). The shrew gets its name from its trunk-like snout.

Despite their name, buffalo weavers do not have any relationship with buffaloes. These birds live in colonies. They build scruffy grass nests in savanna trees and reuse the nests year after year. They protect their territories by screeching a warning call that chases other birds away.

▲ Elephant shrews are the giants of the shrew world.

▲ Under attack, this pangolin will roll itself up into a tight, round ball that bewilders predators.

Serengeti Nights

There are no lights on the Serengeti Plain. Dark is just that—DARK! The only major source of light is moonlight. Yet many creatures feed, hunt, and travel through the darkness. Two of the most interesting are bush babies and pangolins.

Bush babies are related to monkeys and apes. They are small—about the size of a house cat. They get their name from their call, which sounds like a baby crying. Bush babies live in trees in groups called troops. A troop of bush babies feeds, plays, and travels at night. They eat fruit, flowers, and insects.

Pangolins are scaly anteaters. They look somewhat like lizards with large plates or scales covering them from head to tail. Pangolins have long, sticky tongues that can be as long as the animals themselves—about 2 feet (.6 m). They use their tongues to catch ants and termites. Pangolins protect themselves by rolling into tight balls. Predators have been seen rolling a pangolin around, looking for a way to attack it.

Trees and Grasses

❧ Local people laugh about the dangers of the sausage tree. This tree produces fruit measuring about 3 feet (1 m) long and weighing about 11 pounds (5 kg). Visitors are warned to stay away from sausage trees because of potential injuries from falling fruit

or hungry elephants that stampede to eat the "sausages."

Acacias grow beside ponds, where mosquitoes breed. Many years ago, English settlers believed that acacias carried malaria, a disease that causes fever and chills. They did not realize that mosquitoes carried

Hungry elephants can't wait to get a ▶ mouthful of this sausage tree fruit.

malaria. The tree earned the nickname Fever Tree.

Candelabra trees have thick, poisonous sap. People who cut branches must be careful to avoid the sap, which burns skin and blinds eyes. Native people use candelabra branches as cattle fencing. Lions and leopards will not pass through the branches because of the sap.

The Serengeti has three major forms of grass: red grass, pan dropseed, and red dropseed. The red refers to the color of the grass when it is dry. Dropseed grasses are low-lying grasses that survive droughts because of their deep root systems. All three grasses produce large amounts of seeds that attract seed-eating birds and rodents.

Serengeti's Future

The park has suffered the same troubles as most of Africa. Local people are extremely poor. For many years, the poaching of rhinos and elephants for their tusks and horns helped local families survive. Poachers earned more money for one elephant tusk than they could earn in a year of farming. By the 1980s, the elephant population declined to a few hundred. Amazingly, there were only two rhinos left. Poaching had to stop before all the animals were gone.

A worldwide ban on the sale of ivory and rhino horns has helped Serengeti's endangered species regain their population numbers. But poachers

▲ Park rangers have taken this ivory away from poachers.

still kill several thousand animals each year for meat.

Wildlife preserves have been created around Serengeti National Park. These have helped the park in many ways. The preserves serve as a buffer between the park and the local people. They also provide protection for endangered species so that species populations can grow. Today, elephant and rhino herds are growing. The Serengeti—the land that moves on forever—lives.

Chapter Nine

The Human Touch

A Bengal tiger sleeps beside a stream in Royal Chitwan National Park in Nepal. He is a strong male, just over 10 years old. His face and ears bear the scars of earlier fights over territory and females. He measures 8 feet (2.5 m) long and weighs nearly 500 pounds (227 kg).

The tiger is an expert hunter. It is larger than most lions and prefers prey that weighs more than 100 pounds (45 kg). Smaller prey will not

▲ Royal Chitwan National Park in Nepal keeps many endangered animals safe, including this Bengal tiger.

▲ All tiger species are endangered. These young cubs offer hope for a positive future.

feed a tiger that eats 40 pounds (18 kg) of meat or more in a meal. The male eats about 50 deer and wild pigs each year.

Bengal tigers are among the many endangered species of Asia. About 200 tigers live in three protected regions of Nepal. Bangladesh and Bhutan have fewer than 700 Bengal tigers. India's tiger population numbers between 2,750 and 3,750. Tigers have been heavily hunted for their skins and to protect

▲ The Royal Chitwan National Park in Nepal

livestock. Poaching continues to reduce tiger populations in China, Korea, and India.

Threats That Endanger the Land

Threats to grassland biomes are the same on every continent. Loss of habitat to farming and housing is the biggest problem. **Fragmentation** disrupts the ecosystem. Even controlling wildlife populations creates its own set of problems.

When North American settlers crossed the Appalachian Mountains, they found a land of waving grasses and rich soil. Settlers immediately began changing the environment. They plowed through the grass to plant corn and

> **? WORDS TO KNOW . . .**
>
> **fragmentation (frag-muhn-TAY-shuhn)** cutting up a habitat into smaller sections by building roads, canals, railways, and housing

▲ Bison thrive on the prairie land of Waterton Lakes National Park, Canada.

wheat. Farmers planted trees to break the wind. They did not realize that trees do not belong on the prairie.

Settlers and travelers killed pronghorns, bison, and prairie dogs by the millions. In the beginning, the killing provided food and hides to help settlers survive. Once the railroad cut across the land, hunting for sport became popular. Many men shot bison from the com- fort of railroad cars. They had no interest in the meat or hides.

Settlers cut the grasslands into tiny pieces. They built railways and roads to cross the plains. Cattle drives in the 1800s cut wide paths of bare land through former grassland ecosystems.

> **❗ WOULD YOU BELIEVE?**
>
> In 1830, about 30 million to 60 million bison ran wild across the North American prairies. In 1890, only 1,000 wild bison remained. The American Bison Society saved the species from extinction. They set up preserves and private ranches for bison to rebuild their populations.

◀ Neatly arranged farms form a patchwork on former prairie land.

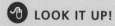 **LOOK IT UP!**

The National Grasslands Program Web site gives a rundown on all national grassland parks. Learn about the program at *http://www.fs.fed.us/grasslands/*.

The Results of Human Actions

Native grasses survive periods of excess rain, drought, and wildfire. Crops do not. At one point, the Great Plains turned into a dust bowl. The land had been misused when native grasslands were converted to cropland. Years of drought prevented crops from growing. The lack of native grass left barren land open to wind erosion.

Tons of rich topsoil blew away, leaving a wasteland behind.

Native grasses spread by both seed and root systems. Fences and fragmentation of grasslands prevented animals from moving through the land.

This story has been repeated in every grassland region in the world. Farming and housing are taking over grasslands. Animals are forced to make way for farms. In Australia, farmers and settlers have killed millions of kangaroos and wallabies. In Africa, it was

▲ A biologist spreads grass and wildflower seeds to restore prairie at Neal Smith Wildlife Reserve in Iowa.

elephants, lions, leopards, and rhinos. On the Russian steppes, it was saiga antelopes.

Efforts to restore natural grasslands are helping to bring back these vast seas of grass and wildflowers. The United States has a National Grasslands Program with 20 government-owned regions. National grassland parks are found across the Great Plains from North Dakota to Kansas. Canada protects tallgrass prairie ecosystems that are thousands of years old.

Similar parks and preserves in Asia, Africa, Australia, and South America keep open plains alive. Worldwide bans on selling animal products, such as ivory and rhino horns, make poaching less attractive. Education about endangered and threatened plants and animals helps them survive. Without these efforts, grasslands would soon become wastelands.

◄ A dust storm erodes topsoil from this Kansas field.

Chart of Species

CONTINENT	KEYSTONE SPECIES	FLAGSHIP SPECIES	UMBRELLA SPECIES	INDICATOR SPECIES
AFRICA	elephants, wildebeests, wild grasses, termites	elephants, lions, black rhinos, white rhinos	elephants, wildebeests, giraffes, zebras, hartebeests	butterflies, grasshoppers, moths, raptors
ASIA	wild yaks, saiga antelopes, great Indian bustards, plateau pikas, hamsters, gerbils	yaks, saiga antelopes, sambar deer	wild yaks, sambar deer, Mongolian wild asses	butterflies, moths, raptors
AUSTRALIA	wild grasses, spinifex, potoroos, kangaroos, wallabies	kangaroos, wallabies, plainswanderers, emus	eastern gray kangaroos, western gray kangaroos, red kangaroos	spinifex, emus, plainswanderers
EUROPE	susliks, wild sheep, wood mice	barn owls, song thrushes, white storks	badgers, barn owls, white storks	swallowtail butterflies, moths, wild orchids, meadow brown butterflies, raptors
NORTH AMERICA	prairie dogs, field mice, bison, antelopes, various wild grasses	black-footed ferrets, swift foxes, burrowing owls	sage grouses, black-footed ferrets, bison, swift foxes	butterflies, moths, grasshoppers, Texas horned lizards, 13-line ground squirrels, field sparrows, Swainson' hawks, raptors
SOUTH AMERICA	maras, pampas grasses, vicuñas, termites	pampas deer, guanacos, vicuñas	Geoffroy's cats, maras, pampas foxes, rheas	Swainson's hawks, pampas deer, raptors

▲ The above chart gives a starting point for identifying key species. Each grassland environment has its own key species. The above chart lists some of those species.

[Bold-faced entries are the ones discussed in the text.]